SURVIVING VIETNAM

SURVIVING VIETNAM

The Writings of One Soldier—
The Feelings of Many

JAMES TOSCANO

SURVIVING VIETNAM
THE WRITINGS OF ONE SOLDIER—THE FEELINGS OF MANY

iUniverse books may be ordered through booksellers or by contacting:

iUniverse
1663 Liberty Drive
Bloomington, IN 47403
www.iuniverse.com
1-800-Authors (1-800-288-4677)

ISBN: 978-1-5320-0910-5 (sc)
ISBN: 978-1-5320-0909-9 (e)

Library of Congress Control Number: 2016918476

Print information available on the last page.

iUniverse rev. date: 12/14/2016

CONTENTS

INTRODUCTION

This book of poems was written by my brother, James Toscano. He was born on October 2, 1946, and passed away on April 23, 2011, at the age of sixty-four from cancer (possibly caused by Agent Orange). Jimmy was smart and talented, played his trombone in the marching band, swam on the swim team, and played on the football team. He was fun loving and, yes, even sometimes mischievous. He always kept us hopping.

Jimmy was the best brother, friend, husband and father anyone could ever ask for and a great soldier. We grew up in a very close-knit and loving Italian family, and he was the only boy of us five kids, right in the middle. I called him my "big brother," my older sisters called him their "little brother," and my mom would lovingly call him her number one son. My dad, his namesake, called him Jimmer.

Jimmy was our rock—and the glue that kept us together. He could always be counted on whenever in need, by all of us, always.

He was drafted to serve in the Vietnam War after attending the University of Minnesota–Duluth campus. He accepted the request from Uncle Sam willingly, even with a bit of excitement. He always was up for a challenge. As a young man of twenty-two, full of life, energy, drive, and determination, he was ready to take on the world to help make it a better place for all of us. And he did!

Rest in peace, dear brother. This book of poems is written by you and compiled for you, and I dedicate it to you and to all who have served in the military.

You are missed by everyone who had the good fortune to meet you and especially by those who had the opportunity to get to know you. We all love you and still feel your strength and compassion from beyond.

With love,
Your "little" sister, Mary Mickelson

1

MOM

My mom looked so happy but also afraid.
Could she so soon see the price her son paid?
At 4:00 a.m. I heard her ask me,
What's out there, son? What do you see?

It doesn't feel right, Mom. The whole house sleeps.
Don't you know at night Charlie creeps?

Want some coffee? Or want to eat?
(Mom knew my mind and soul were beat!)

Someone has to be alert all the time,
I told her (then she knew war must be a crime).
Go ahead, Mom, please go back to bed.
I'll make sure that no one wakes up dead.

She slowly turned and walked away
With tears in her eyes. I knew she did pray
That I could adjust sooner or later
To being back here, no longer a hater.

She'd raised me and taught me all about love,
To believe in God's goodness from up above.
Because I served her God and my country,
She quickly saw the changes in me.

James Toscano

2

COMBAT (B-52S)

Holy shit, What the F was that?
Felt like I got hit with a baseball bat
Right on the side of my head.
But I don't think I'm dead.
My nose is bleeding, see?
Is God now needing *me*?
My ears are ringing; my mind's a blank.
The size of my asshole—I know it shrank!
The ground came up and hit me in the face.
What the F's happening to this place?
Though none bought the farm,
Only the sarge broke his arm.
You know what went down
To us grunts on the ground?
Seems the US Air Force
Got somehow off their course.
You ever want to see B-52s?
Man, for you, have I got news!

3

COMBAT
(AFFECTS BACK HOME)

He felt so cold, his body so stiff.
Might I have saved him—only if?
His name was John, or Tom, I think.
He'd talk about girls back home, then wink!
Both eyes wide open, both lips shut tight,
A dead GI's body is an awful sight.
Oh, I've seen gooks blown wide apart,
But gooks are different; they have no heart.
We'd count the bodies, then cut off their ears.
We hated them; we'd never shed tears.
But load your first buddy onto the meat run,
Then you feel funny. His whole life is really done?
He had a girl and a mom like me.
Is this how they wanted his life to be?
I'll trade him back for me, if I can.
(But then, my mom and girl would lose their man.)
If I (not God) would have to choose
The men to die, the loved ones to lose,
No wonder war is often called sick.
(Winners and losers, so hard to pick!)
Do gooks have girls and mothers and such?
Thoughts like that didn't help my soul much.

4

COMBAT (ALL OVER)

Okay, men, they've run away.
We beat them once again today,
Couldn't have been only two or three.
They were only Charlie or the VC.
We didn't hurt them or they us,
But the last few minutes were a fuss!
Relax now, and smoke if you got them.
Charlie hits and runs, won't return again.
We were thirty, and they were two or three.
It still scared the shit right out of me!
Hoss had the M60 gun a'blazing.
He stood straight up. It was amazing!
Maybe I wasn't cut out for this shit.
My mouth is so dry, I can't even spit.
I got so fucking scared. Know what I mean?
Only there three weeks, I still was green.
They didn't say green, only a cherry.
My face flushed red like a berry.
Then I looked around at each man's face.
Short-timer or cherry, we wanted out of that place!
Okay, men, they're running away.
We beat them back again today.
Only two or three VC—
Maybe two more were in that tree.

5

COMBAT (ON THE SPOT)

I've stared death in the face
In this godforsaken place,
Seen the naked face of horror
On the Laotian border,
Felt terror deep inside,
Wanting to crawl away and hide.
But there is no place to run.
Will this time be the one
That you'll meet your Maker.
You're shaking like a Quaker.
Go ahead and look around.
Pick your face up off the ground!
You ain't dead yet,
But don't place a bet.
The rest of the guys too,
Must feel the same as you.
So make your voice work fast,
Or else this will be the last
Time you'll feel the hot sun.
So start speaking with your gun!

6

FIRST TIME

My loved ones back home are saying prayers.
His family, of course, must be saying theirs.

He's protecting his family, ready to fight.
Funny, so am I.
Can two sides be right?
Who's being told the lie?
But neither him nor I planned to die!
His job was exactly the same as mine:
Defeat your enemy, anyplace, every time.
Of course we wanted to also survive,
But can he and me both stay alive?

Day after night, night after day,
Without any sleep must be the way.
Stare death in the face,
But do not show fear.
Just in case,
Drink lots of beer.
Remember your buddies, who all must
Look at each other full of trust.
Short-timer or cherry, we'll make it here.
Just stay alive for one goddamn year.

If need be, we'll kill him.
We'll blow his ass away.
And it won't even be a sin,
Or so they say.
He'll do it to you and not hesitate.
Whose prayers will be answered?
I'll just have to wait.

Then the big day came,
As I knew it would.
This was not some game.
Lord, this didn't feel good.

Some mother's son
Lies still by my doing.
God—what have I done?
Are you cheering or booing?

His feet were bare.
His "pajamas" were shiny and black.
His face had no hair.
See that big hole in his back?
His skin was so dark,
Even darker than mine.
Look at that scar on his leg.
Was he luckier one previous time?

Yet we were the same,
That gook and me.
I was filled with fear and pain
'Cause I could see
That his God deserted him.
But, funny thing,

My God was gone also.
Now who shall I bring
With me in the rest of the war?
Who'll help me if I must kill once more?

"Outstanding, soldier!" the top kick said.
"The only good gook is one who is dead."

Deep hatred took hold,
Replacing the fear.
His head felt so cold
As we cut off his ear.

So you're the goddamn enemy,
I thought with disgust.
Ashes to ashes, dust to dust.

No God, no family, no friend, and no foe
Went with me from then on, for I only know
That war was a sickness giving medals for gore.
I quietly wished there would be no more.

After lots of beer and lots of wine,
Only then do I begin to feel fine.
Hey, buddy, if you will give me a dime.
I'll tell you about that very first time!

7

GOD'S WISDOM?

As the cherries come
And the short-timers go,
This war will be won.
That I know.

Not the war for this smelly land,
For what is gained when young men die?
Many times have we taken a stand,
Only to bid some good men good-bye.

No, the real battle rages within.
Tell me, oh Lord, isn't this a sin?

You know all and see all. Are you blind?
Is it possible that God, too, can lose his mind?

Thy kingdom come, thy will be done.
Is it me, or are you the crazy one?

Who are you to pick and choose
Those who win and those who lose?

Hippie, Slim, Sergeant King, and I—
Why should I live, why should they die?

Come down here with me on our next firefight.
I'll show you who's wrong; I'll show you who's right.

Prayer is the answer, my mother would say.
I'm glad she can't see what God has done today.

If I make it home, I'll loudly proclaim,
"Mom, your God is not the same

As he was when you were young,
In church as songs to him are sung.

I'll listen not hear; I'll look not see
Your God better do some explaining to me!

James Toscano

8

A Grunt's Poem

Why do I like to be alone?
Why do I call no place home?
Why do I drink so much more than you?
Why do I often feel down and blue?
Why do we look at each other with distrust?
Go ahead, ask me if you must.

Back in nineteen sixty-eight,
I mostly knew love and very little hate.
A youngster of twenty-two was I,
Sometimes too bold and sometimes too shy,
Strong as an ox
And smart as a fox.
UNCLE SAM needs you, so I said okay,
For I was brought up to think that way.
Then far away in Vietnam,
Good-bye boy and hello my man.

To protect and to serve
Took all of my nerve.
Ideals, beliefs, goals, and such
Proved to be a little too much.
This young soldier had to ignore
His heart and soul to survive the war.

Why bother making friends only to see
Many of them taken away from me?
Why play cards, watch them cut the deck—
Next day watch a bullet hit their neck?

What was his name? Where did he call home?
Who knows? Who cares? Leave me alone!
Fear then anger then hatred with a vengeance
Replaced trust and love. Does that make sense?

For too many months the only thing trusted
Was the sound of choppers and a weapon not rusted.
Not enough water to drink—
Did that branch move, or is it a dink?

James Toscano

No showers or shaves
For thirty-eight days.
Brush your teeth then swallow the water.
Comb your hair? Why the hell bother!
Live like an animal, then you will see
What that war did to me.
Of the sweat, the stink, you'll soon get wise.
Live long enough to see one more sunrise.

Close my eyes and sure as shit,
I'll be the next one to get hit.
What's real is death and medevacs
And these rucksacks on our backs.
Green tracers fly overhead.
Zip up the rubber bag; he's dead.

They came and went, my comrades.
A very few had become dads.
I'd watch them change as time went on—
More tired, more quiet, and then they were gone.
At first they'd talk about family and friends,
Then only to God to make amends.

Cars and bars and a bed to sleep in.
I had taken for granted but never again.
Milk and steaks and a dish of ice cream—
All seemed like some faraway dream.

I'm home. I made it, so be advised.
I'll do as I please, even if it's unwise.
Cars and bars and a freedom to roam—
I fought for these pleasures back home.

So do your thing, and let me do mine.
I won't bother you or moan or whine.
I treasure each day that has no more fear.
I need peace and quiet and just one more beer

James Toscano

9

THE FIRST ENCOUNTER

The choppers whap, the rockets scream
The knowledge I'm a part of the team.
The first night I was over here
Filled me up with such a fear.
Rocket attack! Stay down! Incoming!
What next will this war to me bring?
No one was hurt in this first attack,
But I sure wished I could go back
To home, to Canada, or to anywhere
That I could grow old to have gray hair.
The sarge, he was gray. He shouted to me,
"Grab your weapon, boy, and let's go see
If the gooks are in the barbed wire. And
Don't waste ammo until I tell you to fire."

I followed him up front and behold,
The sarge didn't look so very old.
I was twenty-two and he was thirty-three.
I knew then that I would have to be
The best, the bravest, the smartest man,
Or I would go home in a garbage can.

10

WATER AND FEAR

Food, shelter, and something to drink—
Not in that order is how I now think.
With no water for days, you found out quick:
Young and healthy you soon became sick.
A warm, dry place was not within reason
During the monsoon or rainy season.
Then the sun, the heat and humidity
Was also where you didn't want to be.
Why talk about weather? you do ask.
In Vietnam's sunlight, you do not bask.
Just when you stop looking to compare,
Suddenly Charlie would be there.
Mortars would thump; rockets would roar.
You'd stop thinking about food anymore.

Shelter first, then maybe water,
Then ammo. Next food? Why bother?
Food is needed only for the man
Who has shelter, water, and a full ammo can.
Turkey, chicken, and beef pot pies
Are for water and for the man who survives.

11

MEDALS IN GLASS

For hands that kill
The training is good,
So do your will
As any soldier would.
Nothing's wrong, so you're told.
You're the best soldier here,
Though you're getting old.
Vietnam was your best year.
Extend a couple of months
And we'll guarantee
If you're alive, not dead at once,
A hero with medals you can be.

I took my medals and awards of valor
And put them down into the cellar.
Danny and Sissy found them there
And placed them in a glass case so bare.
Loving and caring was their intent;
It put me back into repent.
Thank you, Dan and Sissy. I'm sorry
I smashed the display of intense glory.

12

AMBUSH BY THE NUMBERS

Set up the ambush right now, right here—
Two-man positions not far, not too near.

The company is reduced. I know that's fine.
Instead of eighty, spread out thirty-nine.

No talking, no smoking, no joking at all,
No sleep for me or for anyone at all.

Charlie is coming through here tonight.
We'll wipe his ass out in this little fight.

The gooks are moving, that I know.
Intelligence reports have told us so.

But, sir, S2 has fucked up before.
Do they really understand about this war?

Charlie wasn't supposed to be in the grass.
The last time he almost kicked our ass.

They weren't gooks or untrained VC.
Regular NVA soldiers were waiting for me.

When we called for support from the air,
Only one chopper could find his way there.

Ambush sounds good to West Point lieutenants
Who traded their bars for dormitory pennants.

The books on war were written, you see,
By grunts trying to survive, just like me.

Ambush has two meanings at best.
The gooks may also lay us to rest.

Officers or gentlemen, West Point is okay.
But practice war on someone else today!

James Toscano

13

SPOOKY (USAF)

The tongue of red fire
Was our support last night.
Her minigun's chatter was our choir,
Burping up tracers—oh, such a sight!
The sound of lead flying
At an astounding speed—
I knew gooks were dying.
Even Charlie wouldn't lead
His men into that hail of lead.
They cannot survive; they all are dead!
At morning's rays of yellow sunlight,
We'd saddle up, knowing that last night
The red tongue killed them or scared away
Charlie, but it didn't work out that way.
They did somehow survive our spooky.
Another ambush would get him or get me.
Brave they were or foolish indeed.
Me against them spooky could feed
Tracers and bullets to them to swallow.
They trail me, and the sarge we will follow.

14

HOMECOMING, OR COMING HOME

Fear of the future, fright of the night,
Becomes anger then rage during the fight.

Push panic away, or you will find
That you are surely losing your mind.

Thou shalt not kill, a commandment said.
Forget it here, boy, or you'll be dead!

I want to lay down my M16.
I want to go back to my homecoming queen.

We looked so sharp, her and I.
She wore chiffon; I wore a bow tie.

On the football team, I tried my best.
Will 'Nam be my final place of rest?

The chaperones knew we spiked the punch.
Back then we were a daring bunch.

The real world seemed so far away.
Can I survive just one more day?

Lose the big game, but you'd still know,
Your cheerleaders backed you wherever you'd go.

Look around here. There are no cheers—
Only hot coke, cold blood, and warm beers.

The blood runs warm when first it flows.
It gets cold fast, as every medic knows.

The big days back home like homecoming,
Over here they don't mean a friggin' thing.

Homecoming now seems far away and old.
Will I make it home warm or cold?

15

HEALTHY BODY, SICK MIND

How many times must men go to war
For silver or gold or for iron ore?
The leaders of our great country
Are blind as bats in a cave or a tree.
Stop and think and analyze.
Stop and look at war in their eyes.

When I was twenty-two years of age,
Fighting for a girl I thought was my rage,
I made it back home and thank God
My family was there in soul and bod.

When your war is done, you will find
A lot of strong guys with a troubled mind.
They're tired, they're weak, and so alone.
They need help from you and me and from home.
Precious metals are rare in the USA,
And peace is all for what I do pray.

Kill Charlie for certain and then
The shower curtain you see in life.
Nothing's for certain except strife.
Please let my mind forget where it's been.

16

SHRAPNEL IN MY HEART

I remember when living was such a breeze,
When a cough a snore or a little sneeze
Was something that was taken for granted
And wouldn't attract green tracers of lead.

Three on a match—that phrase from the past—
Never did I know it was some soldiers' last.

Puff of life or death, I guess—
Seems war has always been a mess.

The rules of war were new to me.
The medals, I thought, were great to see.

I won my own but quickly learned
The price you pay for medals you earned.

There was little glory in the war I tasted.
So many fellows' lives were wasted.

Their names are on the granite wall.
Their medals, too, seemed too small.

My name should be on that wall for sure,
But I survived and now must endure.

The pain my heart still feels inside.
How come I wasn't a fellow who died?

17

DOC

Doc the medic didn't believe in war.
He was a conscientious objector.
Doc, at least carry a .45;
It may someday keep you alive.

Nope, not me. Save lives, I will,
But never shall I be able to kill.

At first I thought, What a dumb fool!
Didn't he learn nothing in church or school?
But he served his country oh so well.
He also tasted that man-made hell.
When duty called, he always was there.
No doubt in my mind, Doc did care.
He did his thing, and I did mine.
Never once did I hear him curse or whine.
Doc showed he was brave and very strong.
Unlike me, he never felt he did wrong.
He didn't criticize; he didn't scold.
Like me, he just wanted to someday grow old.
Six months he spent in our company,
Then Doc went home to his church and family.
In his possession, a weapon would rust.
But under Doc's care, we all did trust!

18

SYDNEY

Australia was my R&R.
How I loved the Aussie's bar.
Dark ale and rum was my best friend.
Many a wound would their effect mend.
Ellen or Helen was there indeed.
Warmth and love she knew I'd need.
Her flat was shared with another
Back in 'Nam. Had I seen her brother?
She had lots of beer and a hot-tub bath.
The sidewalk below she called her footpath.
Rest and relax, Ellen said to me.
Enjoy tonight; let yesterday be.
But little could she sense or know
My real fear was for tomorrow.

Bondi Beach was better than heaven.
My R&R days totaled seven.
From beach to her bed, she'd volunteer
To love or to listen or to bring back a beer.
She's teaching schoolchildren, I'm sure, today.
I hope her roomie's brother made it home to stay!

19

COMBAT (TYPE O+)

Panic and confusion—
Doc needs a transfusion.
But we're pinned down.
Attack or hold our ground?
I've got type O.
Should I try to go
Over to Doc? What the heck.
Hooks's got it in the neck.
Look at the blood spurting.
Hooks must be hurting.
So I gave it a try.
Don't ask me why.
But Hooks did fuckin' die.
And I cannot cry!

20

COMBAT (IN BETWEEN)

Resupply, and its about time—
The choppers will be here around nine.
We had two hours to clear the LZ.
Then it's water and food for you and me.
The work went fast, lots of joking.
Hippie saved some joints, and we were smoking
And talking about how we were going to get laid
By that new young gook hooch maid.
Half past nine, they're still not here.
Don't worry; they loaded on extra beer.
Now it was half past ten.
What? They can't make it till when?
Noon tomorrow. What the fuck?
The weather's bad, even for a duck.
Hell with the weather. We'll be damned.
We can move out and the choppers can't?
Seems the mountain air over here
Won't lift the choppers with our beer.
Another day and one more night—
Hope we don't get into a firefight.
Tomorrow the choppers will be a beautiful sight!

21

GIRL BACK HOME

Please write to me, my girl did say.
I'll write to you, Jim, every day.

Write I did, quite faithfully.
And every day she wrote to me.

The first three weeks were not too bad.
I even wrote home to my dad!

This will be a snap, I said, and my dear,
Tell Mom and Dad I'll be back home in a year.

That was way back in 1968,
Before I learned to fight and hate.

I'd rather fill a truck with dead gooks
Than lose one GI, no matter how it looks.

My letters got fewer, and hate took hold.
I traded my love for a heart growing cold.

Reduced to a machine, bent on survival,
As a Screaming Eagle, I learned my job well.

Experience in life and in death I did gain
By closing my heart to love and to pain.

I saved letters from home and from my girl.
Then monsoons and choppers did help uncurl

The knots that tied her close to me.
My letters came home less frequently.

I ran out of good things I could say.
I hoped my girl still knew how to pray!

22

BRANIFF AIRLINES

The big jetliner pushed me back in my seat.
Its wheels left 'Nam; it sure felt neat.
I opened my eyes and did look down
At the godforsaken and hated ground.
Next thing I knew, I saw the sea.
A blonde, round-eyed stewardess said to me,
Coffee, tea, or milk, soldier?
At her eyes I stared and could not answer.
A bottle of scotch was in my bag.
She turned away; she did not nag.
Against the rules, a sergeant did say.
But rules mean nothing to me today.
I was leaving 'Nam; my job was done.
Help yourself, Sarge, you also deserve one.
Joking and laughing, we had our fill.
Then the plane got quiet, full of chill.
Our minds were back into that war.
The sarge said he'd have to go back once more.
Not me, I thought, *my fighting is finally through.*
But Braniff eventually lost her fight too!

23

WHEELS

When I get home, I'll get in my car
And drive it down to the nearest bar.
Never again will I want to walk—
No, not even around the block.
Called grunts or legs, all jokes aside,
I'll never again crawl if I can ride.
I'll build a stock car, and at the track,
It will go so fast I'll never look back.
Humping the mountains or rice paddies,
I'll never again be brought to my knees
In mud, in jungle, or elephant grass.
I'll make them all now kiss my sweet ass.
Driving 90, 100, or 110—even faster—
Slower I'll never be the master
Of my life, for too many times over there
I felt like the tortoise, not like the hare.
Being bogged down, pinned down, was insane.
If I could move quickly, I knew I would gain
The escape I needed so desperately.
Please bring a 'Vette or a Jeep to me!

24

POINT MAN

Walk by point today and for the next week;
The hidden enemy you must seek.
Out front, the ambush you must discover.
Or else some gooks will zap your brother.
They'll let you walk because they know
Forty guys in back are their real foe.
They can drop you on point at their will,
But they'll wait for all your buddies to kill.
The best thing that is going for you
Is that their jungle and mountains ain't brand-new.
The hunting back home with Uncle Tommie
Taught you about trails and woods and now the commie.
Miss a broken branch or a bush looking funny
Then never will the guys hear from their honey.
Charlie sees and hears in his own land.
To him, we sound like a marching band.
Trip wires, booby traps, or bouncing Bettys
Or the wide open spaces of their rice patties—
Stay alert; stay alive, we used to say,
Or in a grave in 'Nam we'll lay!

25

BIRTHDAY 1969

Christmas, New Year's, or President's Day—
They even walked on the moon yesterday.
Over here, each morning starts out the same.
Life and death has become the game.
Cobras, spookies, and our resupplies
Have taken over our lows and our highs.
My birthday was just last week, I think.
Or was that when I killed the last dink?
October second of sixty-nine—
Another birthday would just be fine.
But in the bush, we soon discover
Holidays and birthdays run into each other.
DEROS when I expect to get home,
Then never again will I be so alone.
And then the big day came for sure.
Could I return home to the prayers of her?
I stopped at the plane and looked behind.
The new guys with birthdays were in a bind.
Birthdays, death days, they soon would know,
Were the same for them. I feel so low.

26

FIRST FIREFIGHT

Fear, terror, my first contact—
What the hell happened? Is that a fact?
We were ambushed, bigger than shit.
My M16 got two rounds out of it.
Why it jammed, I soon did know.
Eighteen not twenty rounds in the clip must go.
I hit the turf and then looked around,
Then slammed my face again into the ground.
All the guys looked scared as hell.
Next time I'll do so very well
That they will look up to me
And see what an airborne ranger can be.
We got caught; that's for sure.
I'll carry your radio. Yes, yes sir!
The captain looked and knew at once
That he and I could avoid that dunce
And advance or dig in or flank left and right,
Then blow Charlie to the end of his light.
We all survived that first firefight.
Now who's smarter than Charlie at night?

27

RTO
(RADIO TELEPHONE OPERATOR)

Call for support, the captain said.
Or we'll all for sure be friggin' dead.
Call in our position; we're under fire.
Tell them our situation is dire.
The batteries for the Pric 25
Went dead, but so far we're all alive.
I shut it off for one minute or two.
The battery came back, and we all knew
The next few seconds would mean for us—
Support and supplies or return to dust.
The location, the coordinates, broadcast clear,
Our supplies and support were very near.
The captain, well, he was later found
With his .45 pistol on the ground.
Like him or hate him, we agreed,
The radio working was what we needed.
By his side I did stay
Until the meat wagon took him away.
The lieutenant looked at my radio
And wondered if he was the next to go?

28

STARS TONIGHT

Look up at the stars above.
Each one stands for God's true love.

The moon, the stars, the entire sky
Stand for truth—never a lie.

Then look down at Mother Earth below—
Famine and floods, deserts or mountain snow.

Look close at a country called Vietnam.
Can you tell that something's gone wrong?

So many GIs have met their Maker.
Can stars be bought by the acre?

The heavens looked as good as can be.
Would the next KIA possibly be me?

Remember, Jack, to look around
To Mother Earth. Don't be bound
By people, planets, or by things.
Just relax and see what tomorrow brings.

Do your thing, right or wrong.
Just keep on singing the same old song.

Some day our future will be the best.
Until that time, I'll get some rest.

The time is close, near at hand,
When I will hear heaven's band.

Though with my country I don't always agree,
I'm happy the stars I still can see.

29

MAIL CALL

Letters from home at any time
Made you feel so good and feel so fine.

They didn't know what happened last night,
How your heart stopped beating—too full of fright.

Tell them hi; everything's going fine.
Tell them last night the spaghetti and wine

Tasted so good, like the days of old.
(The wine was warm beer; the spaghetti ice cold.)

They'll write about the good things going on.
You're an uncle, Jim; your sis had a son.
Will my sister's son have to go through this?
I wonder if wars my nephew can miss.

Then look around at the fellow over there—
No letters from home. Don't his people care?

Share some popcorn or cookies with him.
The same places as you, he has been.

Mail call comes so far and between—
No time to answer, you know what I mean?

The bundles of letters, the notes from home—
Read them and smile, and you're still all alone

Tell them it's nothing; you'll survive
This little war and come home alive

To laugh, to cry, and to write letters
To little nephews who are still bed wetters.

But laugh or cry, remember one thing:
The good feelings that those letters did bring.

James Toscano

30

WATER

Monsoon was just a word to me
Before I knew what was to be.
Ten canteens I'd hump on my back
Along with eighty pounds of rucksack.
Ammo and food and letters from home
Were on my back, so I didn't feel alone.
Dry season was something so brand-new—
No water, no showers, no morning dew.
My body stinks; my teeth feel gummy.
My toes, my feet, my crotch feel scummy.
That little scratch on my arm or leg
Never healed right, washing water to beg.
Soap and bandages, we always had some,
But water suddenly had become
More precious than a letter from home.
That sore on my skin—I'd see the bone.
God, let me die like a true man,
Not like a fish in a sardine can.
Ammo and rations, I've got enough.
We need water, not smokes to puff!

31

COME HOME

Baseball, football, or hockey playoffs,
Lockouts, strikes, or industry layoffs

Land men on the moon for all to see,
Or shoot students at Kent State University.

The freedom to pursue your life's goal—
Tycoon or pauper or mining of coal.

Happiness, liberty, a life free of fear,
Wine whiskey, or a six-pack of beer

Your country needs you, Jim, to defend
Her flag, her heritage to the end.

Answer her call—yes, I did indeed.
I knew that Old Glory had a need

To overcome threats to her survival,
To protect her love of the Bible.

Canada was a haven for some.
I answered Old Glory with my gun.

I stepped across the line of induction.
I knew I could handle death and destruction.

Then my world began falling apart,
For country or flag I wanted no part,

The pain and suffering by my own hand!
Only the meek should inherit this land.

Keep your ballgames, your strikes and religion.
Give me only a homing pigeon.

I want to go back to my friends and family.
I only want to return to being me!

James Toscano

32

DEDICATED TO THE KRAUT AND/ OR JANE FONDA (HANOI JANE)

Bomb Hanoi, we used to say.
Chi-Comm was heard every day.
Jane Fonda, who the hell is she?
Has she ever heard of me?
Apologize! To who? For what?
She really is a —— slut
To cuddle with the lying Cong,
To tell them my dead buddies are wrong.
When she gets into my sights,
I'll do my best to put out her lights.
Then funny thing, I saw a flick.
Jane and her dad were stars in it.
Hanoi was far in the past.
On Golden Pond was Henry's last
Time to understand Jane's betrayal.
He knew her well; I knew her little.
Did he feel proud? Did he feel shame?
Now he's dead; now I feel pain.
She lost her dad; I lost some friends.
Will her beliefs bring peaceful ends
To blood and bombs and grief and wars?
Will combat vets stay away from bars?

Was I right? Was she wrong?
Which one of us knew the Cong?
If Jane and I would meet today,
Would I have the guts to say,
Twenty years ago I hated your guts.
Jane, look at me. Are we both nuts?

GLOSSARY

Poem 1: Mom
Charlie: A Vietnamese soldier.

Poem 2: Combat (B-52s)
grunts: US foot soldiers in Vietnam, infantrymen on the ground.
B-52s: US Air Force long-range, subsonic, jet-powered, strategic
bomber from the 1950s.

Poem 3: Combat (Affects Back Home)
GI: US soldiers.
gooks: Term used by US military during the Vietnam War. Most GIs
would simply refer to their enemies as gooks.
meat run: Removing injured or dead soldiers.

Poem 4: Combat All Over
VC: Vietcong soldier.
M60: Officially the US machine gun.
Green: Newly arrived US soldiers in Vietnam.
cherry: Term for new replacement soldiers from the States; also called
fresh meat.

Poem 5: Combat (On the Spot)
Quaker: Member of the Religious Society of Friends. In the past, the
Quakers were known for their refusal to participate in war.

Poem 6: First Time
top kick: First sergeant, head commander.

Poem 7: God's Wisdom?
"Thy kingdom come, thy will be done": From the Lord's Prayer.
God: Name for our Father who art in heaven, our Lord.
hippie: A person whose behavior, dress, and use of drugs were not conventional—sometimes called flower children.

Poem 8: A Grunt's Poem
grunt: US foot soldier.
dink: Vietcong soldier (also gook, Charlie).
medevac: Medical evacuation of wounded or killed soldiers.
green tracers: Color of the Vietcong rockets, which glowed green.
rucksack: Military backpack used to carry needed food, water, ammunition, and supplies.
short-timer: Someone who had spent less than three months in Vietnam.

Poem 9: The First Encounter
choppers: Short for helicopters.
incoming: Take cover, hit the dirt.

Poem 10: Water and Fear
monsoon: Weather phenomena, seasonal downpour of rain with wind changes.

Poem 11: Medals in Glass
glass case: Glass display case (hutch) for trophies, collectables, keepsakes.

Poem 12: Ambush by the Numbers
ambush: Surprise attack, trap, bushwack, sudden attack.
S2: Grumman S2 tracker plane, the first single-airframe warfare aircraft.
NVA: North Vietnamese Army, the people's army of Vietnam.
grunts: Infantrymen in the US military, US foot soldiers.
West Point: Top-shelf training school for officers.

Poem 13: Spooky (USAF)
spooky: The Douglas AC-47, the first in a series of gunships developed in the United States, known for its rapid-fire weapons, constant stream of fire, string of tracers; a.k.a. Puff, the Magic Dragon.
tracers: Bullets or cannon caliber projectiles built with small pyrotechnic charges in their base. Green usually meant incoming; red usually meant outgoing.
gooks: Vietcong soldiers.

Poem 15: Healthy Body, Sick Mind
Charlie: Slang for Vietcong.

Poem 16: Shrapnel in My Heart
three on a match: A superstitious saying stating that if three people light a cigarette from the same match, one will die soon. Smoking was very popular back then and very well accepted in offices, hospitals, elevators, etc.
granite wall: Vietnam Veterans Memorial is a two-acre memorial in Washington, DC, which honors members of the US armed forces who died in service.

Poem 17: Doc
.45: Semiautomatic handgun.
conscientious objector: Someone who does not believe in war or shooting a gun. Doc chose to serve but not to shoot.

Poem 18: Sydney
R&R: Rest and relaxation before heading back to Vietnam.
Aussie's bar: An Australian bar (Australia was one of America's allies)
flat: apartment, a place to live.
footpath: Slang for where prostitutes walked.
'Nam: Vietnam.
Bondi Beach: A popular tourist beach in Sydney, Australia, back then and now.

Poem 19: Combat (Type O+)
type O+: Most common blood type, O positive.

Poem 20: Combat (In Between)
choppers: Helicopters.
LZ: Loading zone.
joints: Hand-rolled marijuana cigarettes, not legal back then but popular with hippies and others to relax, to get high.
firefight: Helicopter missions and combat.

Poem 21: Girl Back Home
gooks: Vietcong soldiers.
GI: US foot soldier, infantryman.

Poem 22: Braniff Airlines
Round-eyed stewardess: Used by Asians to describe Americans.
my fighting is through: Jim had already extended his tour and was finally heading home.

Poem 23: Wheels
stock car: An ordinary car that is modified for racing. Jimmy did come home and did get a chance to race his stock car very fast.
hump: March or hike carrying rucksacks.
'Vette: Short for Corvette.

Poem 24: Point Man
walk point: Man taking the lead through Vietnam brush.
commies: Term for Vietcong. The Communist Party of Vietnam (CPV) is the founding and ruling party of the Socialist Republic of Vietnam.
bouncing betties: Mines that, when triggered, launch into the air and detonate at waist height.

Poem 25: Birthday 1969

birthday 1969: Author was twenty-three years old on October 2, 1969.

walked on the moon yesterday: Apollo 11, July 20, 1969 (Jim's sister's eighteenth birthday, while her brother was in Vietnam). On that mission, Neil Armstrong was the first human to walk on the surface of the moon.

DEROS: Date eligible to return from overseas.

Cobras, spookies: Douglas AV 47, US Air Force gunship.

Bell AH-1 Cobra: Two-blade attack helicopter.

Poem 26: First Firefight

M16: Assault rifle adopted by the US Army in 1964 and considered one of the best assault rifles in the world in 1969.

airborne ranger: Highly trained soldier.

Poem 27: RTO (Radio Telephone Operator)

RTO: Radio telephone operator, someone experienced who wouldn't get rattled under fire. If an officer got hit, RTO would take command, calling for fire, medics, backup, or support. It was a dangerous job.

Pric 25: Backpack radio, a piece of military electronics that was the size and weight of a case of soda.

meat wagon: An ambulance or any other emergency vehicle used for medical evacuations.

Poem 28: Stars Tonight

KIA: Killed in action.

Poem 29: Mail Call

mail call: Letters from home delivered to soldiers fighting overseas.

Poem 30: Water

hump: To march, to carry from one location to another uphill/ downhill, with supplies and full rucksacks on backs.

rucksack: Army backpack for supplies.

Kent State: Kent State University in Ohio. Unarmed college students doing a peaceful antiwar protest against the Vietnam War were shot by the Ohio National Guard on May 4, 1970. Four died and others were wounded.

Poem 31: Come Home

only the meek shall inherit the land: A reference to the third verse of Jesus's Sermon on the Mount. In the King James Version of the Bible, the text reads, "Blessed are the meek, for they shall inherit the earth."

Poem 32: Dedicated to the Kraut and/or Jane Fonda (Hanoi Jane)

Kraut: German.

Chi-Comm: Two-way radios used for communication.

Jane Fonda: A US citizen who aided and abetted the enemy during the Vietnam War. She called our POWs (prisoners of war) hypocrites and baby killers and said they lied about being treated poorly by the Vietnam as prisoners of war. She called our men liars publicly and is known for putting down Vietnam vets and for stating that they should apologize for their actions in Vietnam. She also posed with the Vietcong and enemy on their tanks, hence the nickname Hanoi Jane.

On Golden Pond: A 1981 romance movie starring Katharine Hepburn, Henry Fonda, and Jane Fonda.

Miscellaneous:
Zippo: A brand of lighter most commonly carried during the war. Some Vietnam soldiers inscribed sayings on them.

A saying....
You have never lived till you almost died. For those who fight for it, life has a flavor the protected will never know. -author unknown-

CONCLUSION

Mary Mickelson, the poet's sister

Like most Vietnam veterans, my brother, Jimmy, didn't talk much about what went on over there. He did, however, share a few stories with me from time to time, and I would like to conclude with one of those.

He said, "Little sis, sometimes you have to take a chance, use your brains, and do what your gut tells you to do, even though you are not sure what the outcome may bring." (He was helping me make an important life decision. I was glad my big brother was there for me to lean on.)

He told me a story then about a time when he was in Vietnam. He was selected as the radio operator for his company. Jimmy had the responsibility of being the contact person, communicating from the jungles of Vietnam to headquarters in order to get orders. The heavy bag phone was all he had for communication.

While on a mission, they got ambushed by the Vietcong. Snipers were everywhere, hiding behind bushes, up in the trees, behind rocks, and even in ditches. The Vietcong were not supposed to be in that area, and yet there they were, attacking.

My brother called in for permission to fire, which was proper procedure. The response was "There are not suppose to be Vietcong in that area, according to our information. Hold your fire. We will respond as quickly as we can, when we are certain it is the Vietcong."

The attackers were getting closer. They were all over the place. The soldiers were sitting ducks. Still no response. A decision to fire had to be made right then and there.

The soldiers kept looking at my brother for the signal to fire. He was still waiting for the urgent command. He looked at the radio; he looked at the men; he looked back at the radio. He paused for a moment, and then, looking back at the men, yelled, "Fire!" They returned the fire and got the snipers.

A short while later, after the dust cleared, the response from headquarters finally came through. Headquarters said that, yes, there were Vietcong in that area, and, yes, permission to fire was granted. So my brother said, "Thank you, sir!" He waited for a moment or two and then said, "Bang, bang! Got them, sir!"

He may have saved many lives that day. He helped his men by taking a chance and doing what his gut told him to do and what he thought was the right thing to do—the same way he helped me while I was growing up and helped everyone who knew him.

Thank you for being you, big brother. You are missed by many.

James Toscano

Printed in the United States
By Bookmasters